SEX DRUGS ROCK & ROLL

ALSO BY ERIC BOGOSIAN

Talk Radio

Drinking in America

ERIC BOGOSIAN

SEX DRUGS ROCK & ROLL

HarperCollins*Publishers*

Originally produced on the New York stage by Frederick Zollo and Robert Cole in association with 126 Second Ave. Corp. and Sine/D'Addario Ltd., Ethel Bayer, and William Suter.

CAUTION: Professionals and amateurs are hereby warned that *Sex, Drugs, Rock & Roll* is subject to a royalty. It is fully protected under the copyright laws of the United States of America, and of all countries covered by the International Copyright Union (including the Dominion of Canada and the rest of the British Commonwealth), and of all countries covered by the Pan-American Copyright Convention and the Universal Copyright Convention, and of all countries with which the United States has reciprocal copyright relations. All rights, including professional and amateur stage performing, motion picture, recitation, lecturing, public reading, radio broadcasting, television, video or sound taping, all other forms of mechanical or electronic reproduction, such as information storage and retrieval systems and photocopying, and the rights of translation into foreign languages, are strictly reserved.

All inquiries concerning rights should be addressed to William Morris Agency, Inc., 1350 Avenue of the Americas, New York, NY 10019, Attention: George Lane.

FIRST EDITION

Designed by Alma Orenstein

Library of Congress Cataloging-in-Publication Data
Bogosian, Eric.
Sex, drugs, rock & roll / Eric Bogosian.—1st ed.
    p.   cm.
"Originally produced on the New York stage by Frederick Zollo and Robert Cole in association with 126 Second Ave. Corp. and Sine/D'Addario Ltd., Ethel Bayer, and William Suter."
ISBN 0-06-016600-2
I. Title. II. Title: Sex, drugs, rock and roll.
PS3552.O46S4   1991   90-55565
812'.54—dc20

---

91 92 93 94 95 CC/HC 10 9 8 7 6 5 4 3 2 1

This book is dedicated to the memory of
my fellow artists taken so young by
the plague, AIDS.

CONTENTS

CONTENTS

ACKNOWLEDGMENTS

Before anyone else, myself included, Jo Bonney maintained a vision for this piece. Although I have learned to dislike the idea of "collaboration," I must consider Jo not only my director but coauthor. When I said, "This is good enough," she said, "No, it's not." When I said, "I can't," she said, "You can." Thank you, Jo.

For almost ten years now Fred Zollo has stood by me as producer, and as my friend for more than twenty. Fred has guaranteed that my productions are of the highest quality. I get the best, and the audience benefits. Thank you, Fred.

Special thanks to Tom Miller for his advice and support in the construction of this book.

I would also like to thank Nick Paleologus, Robert Cole, Robert Brustein, John Arnone, Jan Kroese, Jan Nebozenko, Mark Russell, Hal Luftig, Walt Taylor, all my lovely "angels," and the crew for the show at the

Orpheum. Also thanks to my heroic producers at SBK records.

Thanks to Pat Sosnow, the best stage manager in the whole world.

Thanks to Phil Rinaldi, the best publicist in the whole world.

Thanks to George Lane for knowing what to do and when to do it. Thanks to Ron Taft for inspiration and incentive. "No surrender, no return."

Thanks to Performance Space 122, New York City, and the American Repertory Theater, Cambridge, for making me feel at home when *Sex, Drugs* was in its infancy.

INTRODUCTION

According to myth, Alan Freed, a New York deejay, coined the term "rock and roll." But Freed did more than name a phenomenon and introduce it to millions. He also managed to be the center of a scandal, ruin his life with booze, and die young. He was rock and roll incarnate.

The phrase "sex, drugs, rock & roll" has been tattooed onto my life for the past twenty-five years. In fact, for a long time I thought "sex, drugs, rock & roll" was life itself. Anyone not moving at ninety mph with the music blasting was not alive. If you didn't rock, you were dead.

In fact, it's been the other way around. Drugs and AIDS have killed many people, many friends. The phrase "sex, drugs, rock & roll" doesn't have the same party feeling it had fifteen years ago. At times it evokes a danse macabre.

And yet, my whole life and art have marched to the rock beat. The best in life *is* energetic, free, and antagonistic. If you don't go all the way, it's not worth going. My way of thinking was shaped by Dylan and Hendrix and Lennon and Morrison and the rest of the Saints of the Church of Rock twenty years ago, and I am a true believer. I stand by the idealism of rock and roll; I don't think it's something I will outgrow.

And yet . . . rock is offensive too: the macho rock stars gripping their phallic guitars and microphones, the groupies, the piles of money, the greed of promoters and producers, the waste and the wasted, the hypocrisy.

And the house philosophy can be almost ridiculous: "Tune in, turn on, drop out." "If it feels good, do it." "Freedom's just another word for nothing left to lose." "Wanna die before I get old."

One day I put on a shirt with a picture of Che Guevara on it. The next day I put on a shirt with the slogan "Stoned Again"!

I've spent most of my life stuck between idealism and hedonism, between selfishness and selflessness, between love and sex, between chaos and clarity.

Today, in 1991, the question is: how can I be irresponsible at the same time I'm being responsible? Being energetic and radical is wonderful; but if I'm nothing more, I'm a child. A responsible life is more than bumper stickers, T-shirts with slogans on them, and benefit concerts. Social concerns voiced over and over again become hollow when they don't initiate real action.

So I think: "I'm getting older—of course I'm going to be thinking more conservatively. . . ."

But that's bullshit. There's no reason why getting older has anything to do with becoming more conservative. It's more like my brain is finally clearing up the morning after the big party. I can see things don't make sense. And I'm not just "talkin' 'bout my generation." I'm talking about being American.

America is the land of overconsumption that loves to cry for the less fortunate of the world. America wants to be the strongest warrior and the ultimate peacemaker. America wants to live in piggish splendor and be ecologically responsible. America wants to have the highest principles but win the popularity contest. America loves itself and loves to beat itself up. America is schizoid.

Our highest moral values are repeated over and over again as messages in the mass media chorus. But we mock these values, whether they be charity or truth or love or even cleanliness. Benefit concerts are sponsored by beer companies. Our President knows it's not *what* he says that counts but how he *looks* saying it. A free press is poisoned by pornography. We carefully recycle our cans and bottles, ignoring the acid skies and the oil-slick shores.

As a nation we sit at a huge rock concert, singing along to some well-known anthem of cloying sentiment. We love the feeling, the togetherness, the righteousness of the cause. As we watch the evening news or read the daily tabloids, we are shocked together, we are pleased together, we are entertained together, we are saddened together. Unfortunately, when the concert's over, we get back in our cars, drive home, and go to bed. It's only rock and roll.

The urge to be everything at once, to be everywhere at once, to feel everything at once, and to do it as one monolithic group lays the foundation for a nation's neurosis. It is the point of view of a child. It is the point of view of the rock culture on which I grew up. It is my point of view.

This conflict has infected every area of my life. My own need to "do the right thing" as a friend, as a parent, as an artist, as a lover, and as a citizen battles my need to be a big baby. The result is paralysis with a coating of guilt.

I write about those things I can't figure out. The monologues in *Sex, Drugs, Rock & Roll* are my open meditation on the conflicts in my life. They are an attempt to take the nasty sides of myself and put them out there for everyone to see.

My solos work off the attitudes that drive me. These attitudes are hard for me to explore. I uproot them and turn them over as devil's advocate. I take a good look at myself by grabbing the disturbing traits and personifying them in a character. Live performance in front of an audience charges up the examination, raises the stakes. Then I slam one character up against the next and hope that some kind of meditation will evolve. Provocation in the guise of a good time.

I could have titled the show *Conflicts and Meditations on My State of Mind in America in 1990*. But then the theater would have remained empty. You wouldn't have picked up this book. *Sex, Drugs, Rock & Roll* is a provocative title. It promises fun and excitement. We all want satisfaction. There's also the dark side. I hope you enjoy it.

SEX, DRUGS,
ROCK & ROLL

(Lights go down.
An amplified voice is heard. A raucous
deejay.)

Hey, you're listening to WRXX, the
home of hard rock and roll! I don't know
about you, but I want to *party,* I want to rock
the house, I want to take care of business—if
you know what I mean, and I hope you do!
So buckle your belts, grab your hats, zip your
pants, and hoist your bats—we got some
rockin' to do too-night!

(Amplified hard rock blasts at the
audience.
A man appears in silhouette, holding
a stick.

*He begins a frenzied "air guitar"
mime to the music.*

*The lights change. The man is
hobbling toward the audience on the
stick. . . .*

Segue . . .)

GRACE OF GOD

*(A man is revealed hobbling on a cane, holding
an empty paper cup; he addresses the audience.)*

Good afternoon, ladies and gentlemen. I only
want a few minutes of your time. It doesn't cost you
anything to listen. Please be patient with me.

I just got released from Riker's Island, where I was
unjustly incarcerated for thirty days for acts I committed during a nervous breakdown due to a situation
beyond my control. I am not a drug addict.

This is the situation: I need your money. I could
be out robbing and stealing right now; I don't want to
be doing that. I could be holding a knife up to your
throat right now; I don't want to be doing that. . . . And
I'm sure you don't want that, either.

I didn't choose this life. I want to work. But I
can't. My medication costs over two thousand dollars

a week, of which Medicaid only pays one-third. I am forced to go down to the Lower East Side and buy illegal drugs to stop the pain. I am not a drug addict.

If you give me money, if you help me out, I might be able to find someplace to live. I might be able to get my life back together. It's really all up to you.

Bad things happen to good people. Bad situations beyond my control forced me onto the streets into a life of crime. I won't bore you with the details right now. But if you don't believe me, you can call my parole officer, Mr. Vincent Gardello. His home number is 555-1768.

The only difference between you and me is that you're on the ups and I'm on the downs. Underneath it all, we're exactly the same. We're both human beings. I'm a human being.

I'm a victim of a sick society. I come from a dysfunctional family. My father was an alcoholic. My mother tried to control me. My sister thinks she's an actress. You wouldn't want the childhood that I had.

The world is really screwed up. Things get worse every day. Now is your chance to *do* something about it . . . help out somebody standing right in front of you instead of worrying about South fuckin' Africa ten thousand miles away. Believe me when I tell you God is watching you when you help someone less fortunate than yourself, a human being, like me.

I'm sorry my clothes aren't clean. I'm sorry I'm homeless. I'm sorry I don't have a job. I'm sorry I have to interrupt your afternoon. But I have no choice, I have to ask for help. I can't change my life—you can. Please, please look into your hearts and do the right thing! . . . Thank you.

(He addresses people in the front row, begging to one or two while holding out his cup, saying "Thank you very much, God bless you" repeatedly. If money is given, he says, "Stay guilty." If money is withheld, he says, "I really feel sorry for you, man." Finally, he leaves, repeating over and over again, "Thank you, God bless you" . . . segueing into the "Thank you"s that begin the next piece.)

BENEFIT

*(The "thank you"s from the last segment
introduce this segment as a man addresses an
imaginary "host" onstage, then seats himself in
a chair stage left. His accent is "British.")*

Thank you, Bill, thank you. . . .

(Sits, attaches lavaliere microphone to shirt)

Yes, yes, yes, yes, yes, yes . . . we're very excited
about the success of the new album. It's nice having a
number-one album again, you know, considering the
band really hasn't done anything for about ten years
. . . it's a real breath of fresh air. . . .

*(Picks up a glass of water from a small table on
his left, sips the water)*

No . . . I don't, Bill . . . and I'm glad you asked me that question. . . .

(Returns the glass of water and picks up a pack of cigarettes and a lighter; taps out a cigarette as he speaks)

I used to do quite a few drugs. . . . But you know, Bill, drugs are no good for anybody. I've seen a lot of people get really messed up on drugs, I've seen people die on drugs. . . .

(Lights cigarette, inhales deeply)

I was saying to Trevor just the other day—I said, "Trevor, how is it that we managed to survive?" After Jimi died and Janis died and John died, I said to myself, "Why didn't *we* die?" We shoulda died. All the stuff we used to do.

Yes, Bill, I was. I was a bona fide drug addict. I used drugs every single day for five years.

What was it like? Well, I tell you, Bill. I used to get up every morning, before I even brushed my teeth, I would smoke a joint. While I was smoking the joint,

I'd pop a beer. While I was sipping the beer, I'd cook up a spoon of cocaine, heroin—whatever was lying around. Shoot it right into my arm, get completely wasted. . . . Flip on the telly, get high some more . . . maybe order up some lunch . . . have some girls over, get high with them . . . fool around with the girls, get high some more.

I did that every single day for five years.

It was horrible . . . it was horrible. . . . I mean, it was wonderful too, in its own way. I won't lie to you, Bill—my life is based on honesty today.

Yes, we did . . . we saw many tragic consequences. People very close to us. We had a sound engineer who had major problems with drugs . . . Hoover, we called him. His problem was that he wasn't just our sound engineer, he was also in charge of getting the drugs for the band, because we always used to get very high whenever we cut an album. And I'll never forget, we were cutting the *Wild Horses* album, and Hoover shows up—

Oh, thank you, Bill . . . yes, it is a great album. A real rock classic.

—So we're cutting *Wild Horses*, and Hoover shows up with a coffee can full of the most amazing white flake Peruvian cocaine . . . absolutely pure, very wonderful. . . . I don't know if you've ever done white flake Peruvian, Bill, but it's an experience.

Wouldn't mind having a little bit of it right now! *(Laughs out loud, then remembers the audience)* Just joking, just joking!

So we took that can of cocaine, dumped it onto a table in the middle of the studio, cut out some lines two, three feet long. . . . Hoover would do three or four in each nostril . . . what a beast. Don't know where he had room in his skull for the stuff.

And we started to play. . . .

Of course, in those days we didn't just do coke. We did everything—it was heaven! Trevor was smoking Afghani hash round the clock. Nigel was in his crystal meth period, so we had that. Ronnie showed up with a large bottle of NyQuil. We were blind, we were so high . . . completely wasted.

And we started to play, and you know, Bill, we never played better. It was like we all had ESP; it was historic. . . . Myself, I looked down at my fingers and I'm thinking, "It's not me playing this guitar, it's not me playing this guitar. It's God playing." . . . It was awe-inspiring.

(Long pause, loses his train of thought) What was I talking about? . . . Oh right—Hoover!

So we're playing this brilliant music for about an hour, and I happened to look up and there's Hoover in the sound booth, and well . . . he was smashing his head up against the glass. Blood is running down off his forehead all over his nose. His nose is all red with blood. Cocaine is shooting out of his nostrils onto his beard. His beard was all white. He looked like a deranged Sandy Claus.

Well, see, the thing is, the thing is, he forgot to push the "record" button. And he went completely stark raving mad. They had to take him away in a straitjacket. Took him to a sanitarium.

And the sad thing is, Bill, he was one of my closest friends in the whole world.

(Puts out cigarette)

What's that? . . . No . . . no . . . I don't know where he is today. I know he's somewhere. Probably still in an institution somewhere. . . . Maybe he's watching right now.

Hoover, if you're watching . . . *(Makes a thumbs-up gesture to an imaginary TV camera, then laughs)*

You see, Bill, that's the insidious thing about drugs—you don't realize . . . uh . . . I mean, you're having such a good time, you don't realize what a bad time you're having.

I got straight while I was on tour. Woke up one morning . . . typical tour situation: luxury hotel room, I don't even know where I am . . . beautiful naked girl lying next to me in the bed, I don't know who she is, I don't know how she got there . . . champagne bottles all over the floor, cocaine on every horizontal surface. I hardly have the strength to pick up my head. So I pick up the remote control and I flip on the telly.

And I was saved, Bill, I was saved.

You have a man on in this country, on TV all the time. Saved my life. White hair. A genius . . . Donahue, Donahue was on. . . . What he said really hit me. He said: "If you haven't met your full potential in this life, you're not really alive." The profoundness struck me like a thunderbolt. I thought, "That man is talking about me. He's talking about me."

Because here I was, young, talented, intelligent, wealthy, good-looking, very intelligent . . . and what am I doing with my life? I'm on drugs, day and night. I mean, I can understand if you're talking about some Negro guy or Puerto Rican guy in the ghetto on drugs—I can understand that. But in my case it was such a tragedy when you think about it. Such a waste of human potential. Such a waste.

Because, Bill, you can have your caviar breakfast,

lunch, and dinner, you can have your stretch limousines, your Concorde flights back and forth to London. Wads of cash, everyone treating you like God. Women willing to do whatever you want them to do . . . wherever you want them to do it. House in London, house in L.A., apartment in New York . . . home in the Bahamas . . .

Bill, if it doesn't mean anything, what's the point? You know what I'm saying?

Maybe not.

I straightened up and I went cold turkey. Had all my blood changed. And I feel like I've been reborn. I can say today, "I like myself today. I'm not such a bad guy, in fact, I'm an amazingly wonderful human being." I'm honest enough to say that today. I've really come to terms with my own brilliance—it's not a burden anymore.

The rest of the band got straight too, and today, we're just one big happy family. We just want to help other people.

Yes, yes . . . Well, that's why we're doing the benefit to aid the Amazonian Indians. I think they're Indians . . . the people down there in the Amazon . . . that we're helping . . . in the jungle . . . whatever. . . .

Yes! Well, Trevor has a home down in Rio, we go

there every winter when it's summer down there. He has this lovely houseboy takes care of the house for him—Nacho, we call him. He's actually not a boy; he's about fifty or so . . . lovely little guy, very brown, always smiling, very helpful.

Nacho knew we were into the environment, so he hired a boat to take up the Amazon, take a look at the birds and the trees and the flowers and all that shit. . . . So we're going along in this boat and we come to a turn in the river and there was this clearing, turned out it was an Indian village . . . whatever, and we all got out and took a walk around.

Bill, I've never seen such depressing poverty . . . the children running around barefoot with the dogs in the dirt, they have no shoes . . . the women, half naked, breast-feeding their infants straight from their breasts. . . . No running water. Couldn't even get a glass of water. I was parched. No Coke, no Pepsi.

The chief of the whole village came out to greet us. Man owned no clothing whatsoever. Completely naked—everything's showing, his willy hanging out and everything. All he had on was this carved piece of wood on his head with a feather sticking out.

Couldn't even speak English. It was heartbreaking.

I turned to Trevor and I said, "Trevor, we have to do something about this. We have to help these people.

It's up to us, after all—'We are the world,' so to speak."

And so we decided to do the benefit. Now, I hate to say this, but so many of these benefits, they're just ego trips. They raise the money and just throw it at these people. Well, these poor buggers are primitive people—they've never seen money before. They don't know what to do with money. We found when we were down there that there were many things we had they really liked: digital wristwatches, Sony Walkmans, cigarette lighters, cigarettes . . . they love cigarettes.

So we're going to be buying these things for them up here with the money. Shipping them down. Try to improve their lives in a substantial way. Do some good for a change.

Thank you, Bill, thank you. It's nothing. . . .

So I hope everyone watching can tune in when we're on MTV. Brought to you by Kronenbrau Beer, Remington Cigarettes. . . . Have to say it, Bill, have to say it—sorry! The cigarette people have been fantastic, donated a truckload of cigarettes to hand out to the Indians. . . . Or buy the album when it comes out. And remember that for every dollar you donate, fully twenty percent goes directly to the Amazonian Indians.

Bill, I'd like to say one more thing about drugs if I may.

A lot of the kids watching right now buy our albums, learn the lyrics, memorize them, live their lives by them. So I know that everything I have to say is very, very important. And I'd like to say this about drugs:

(He looks directly and "meaningfully" at the audience.)

I've done a lot of drugs. I had a lot of adventures on drugs. Some of my music has been inspired by drugs. In fact, I think it's safe to say I had some of the best times of my life on drugs.

That doesn't mean *you* have to do them.

We were recently invited to the White House to do a special concert for Vice-President Quayle and his lovely wife, Marilyn.

Oh, yes, she's hot . . . she's very hot. *(Aside)* I'll tell you a little story when we get off the air. . . .

He's a wonderful man who, whatever you think of him publicly, in person is a very caring, very sensitive, very intelligent man.

He shared something with us that I would like to share with all of you tonight: The next time someone offers you drugs, remember you can always just . . . turn them in.

Thank you, Bill. Good night.

(Stands and gives the peace sign)

Cheers.

(Walks off)

DIRT

(A man shuffles and rants, scratching and coughing, grumbling in a gruff derelict's voice.)

Fuckin' ya shit fuck piss, ya shit fuck piss, ya shit fuck piss . . . *(Coughs and spits, points at the ground)* What's that? What's that? It's shit, that's what it is. . . . Shit on the ground, shit in the air, it's a bunch of shit if you ask me! You know what I'm talking about, you know what I'm talking about—we're living in a human garbage can, that's what I'm talking about . . . we're living in a human sewer. . . .

(Back to the audience, he picks at the crack in the seat of his pants, talking continuously.)

You can't walk down the street without stepping in some garbage, some dog mess, lumps and smears everywhere ya go . . . some cat piss . . . everything's drenched in piss. Pools of piss. Streams of piss. Rivers of piss. Rivers . . . rivers, the rivers!

The rivers are polluted. They are! You know what I'm talking about. . . . And where do the rivers come from, huh? They come out of the mountains, and the mountains are full of hikers and hunters and cross-country skiers. What are they doing? Pissing on every tree, shitting behind every bush. What do they care? Trees are gonna die from the acid rain anyway!

But you know what happens? You know what happens?

(He indicates his storytelling with a kind of energetic mime.)

The acid rain, the acid rain runs down the tree and mixes with the piss and it makes a little brook and the little brooks flow into little streams. And the streams— where's the stream go, huh? Streams go down by the condos, where the pipes come out filled with more piss and shit and soap suds and tampons and puke from the drunken parties they have on Saturday night 'cause the houses are so ugly they have to be drunk just to live in 'em.

And the streams pour into the rivers and the rivers go by the factories, where they got bigger pipes spewing out chemicals and compounds and compost and arsenic and . . . and NutraSweet . . . and all that goes into the river.

And then the river gets bigger and it goes by the *city*, where they got even bigger pipes choked with all the slop from millions of toilets and garbage disposals and hospital bed pans and laundromats and car washes and fried-chicken places and pizza parlors and whorehouses and Ukrainian restaurants. . . . And all this goes into the river, and the river goes down to the ocean.

And the ocean! What's the ocean? The ocean is just one big oil slick with all this shit being poured into it. But if that isn't enough—no, no, no . . .

(Scratches and coughs)

. . . they gotta drag out these giant garbage scows filled with tons of burning plastic bags of garbage— they drag those around for a couple of months until they stink and are full of maggots and mildew and dump those in too.

And then rich guys ride around in their pleasure boats with their fishing poles and they're drinking their beers and getting drunk and throwin' the empties over the side and pissing over the side and then they get seasick and puke up their steak tartare and caviar and crème brulée and their pâté! *(He pretends to vomit over the edge of the stage.) Braaaaaahhhhhhh!!!!!* And all this stuff is going into the water!

And what else is in the water? Huh?

Fishies, that's what.

Millions and millions of little fishies are swimming around trying to get past the chicken bones and the orange peels and the syringes, and the little balled-up pieces of toilet paper floating by get stuck in their eye! They can't even see, there's so much stuff down there!

And they want to wipe their eyes but they can't 'cause they don't got hands, they got fins. . . . So they go up to the top of the water to look around and they get all covered with oil and it goes in their gills and their hair and they get all greasy and they drown. . . .

And this seagull is flying by and he sees this greasy little fish floating there, so he comes down to get a free meal . . . oooops! Now he's stuck in the oil too! And then a seal, he sees the seagull, now he's stuck in the oil too, he drowns! Then the polar bear, he sees the seal, comes to eat him, he's stuck in the oil too! Then . . . then the lion comes to eat the polar bear, he gets stuck in the oil too. . . .

And there you have it! That's the ocean: just a giant vat of oil, garbage, and dead animals . . . just sloshing around there.

And then a hurricane comes. Then a tidal wave

comes. And the whole mess splashes all over the beaches.

And there you've got it. That's it. Millions and millions of dead fishes all over the beaches. . . .

(Pause)

And then you know what happens?

The rats come, the rats come and they eat the fishies . . . and then, then the cats come and they eat the rats! And then the dogs come and they eat the cats! And then the dogs—you know what the dogs do?

You know what they do! They shit all over the place, that's what they do!

Dog shit, horse shit, pigeon shit, rat shit. You can't go down the street without steppin' in something! *(Mumbling)* Fuckin' shit fuck piss. Shit fuck piss . . .

(He notices something on his foot, scrapes his foot on the edge of the stage.)

We're living in a human cesspool, we're living in a human septic tank. Living in a human toilet.

You know what I say? Flush the toilet, that's what I say! Flush the toilet! Flush the toilet!

That's what I say!

(He hobbles upstage, back to the audience.)

That's what I say . . .

(In the darkness, he vomits.)

BRAAAHHHHHHHHHGGGGGH!

THE STUD

(A man speaks directly to the audience in a slow, easygoing drawl. He's drinking from a long-necked beer bottle.)

Sometimes, when I'm in a bar, having a drink with some fellas, one will make an idle comment like "How does that guy do it? He always gets the girls!"

I remain quiet when I hear such remarks. I like to keep a low profile with regard to my "extracurricular activities." I don't need to advertise. I know what I've got. And the ladies . . . hell, they know better than I do.

I'm not so good-lookin'. I was athletic when I was younger, but I'm no Mr. Universe. I'm medium height, medium weight. Never really excelled at anything, certainly not school. As far as my job goes, they can all screw themselves.

But you know what? I don't give a shit. 'Cause I've got what every guy—and every woman—wants. And all the looks, brains, money in the world can't buy it.

I'm "endowed."

(Takes a swig from his bottle)

I've got a long, thick, well-shaped prick. The kind girls die for.

You're laughing. So what? Fuck you. Facts are facts. I'll hang out in some bar down on Wall Street around six o'clock, and in they all come, the guys with their health-club bodies and expensive Italian suits. Trying to compensate. The women—smart, fresh, pretty. I especially like the ones with the big bow ties and the Adidas sneakers.

I pick out the prettiest one in the room. We start talking about this or that. I act like I'm going to buy her a drink, then save myself the money and say: "Why don't we get the hell out of here?"

Two hours later, I'm in some strange bedroom, blowin' smoke rings at the ceiling.

(He takes a swig from the bottle, puts it down on the floor.)

They love to tell me about their boyfriends and husbands. What wonderful men they are. So nice, so gentle, so dependable . . . so boring.

And they love to tell me what a wonderful cock I've got. So big, so hard, so unlike anything they've got at home. And they love to beg for more . . . and I love to give it to 'em.

Ever see a girl cry 'cause she's so happy? Ever have a girl beg to tear your clothes off? Every see a woman faint because she's had such an intense orgasm?

(Scans the audience as if looking for an answer)

I have.

It's like in school—that Greek guy—what was his name?—Plato, said everything in the world has a perfect example after which it is modeled. That's my sex life. Platonic perfection.

I know what you're thinking. This guy is pretty screwed up. He's lonely. He's obsessed. He's got no love in his life.

Don't tell me about love. I got love. I always keep the choicest for a daily visit . . . that's love. Right? Same as you, same as everybody.

But the point is, I got love, and I got all the others

too. I see a girl walkin' down the street, I like the way she smiles—bingo, she's mine.

Some of 'em get scared after a while, go back to their boyfriends. That's fine with me. I understand—it's a lot to handle. Some get addicted, I get rid of them too.

But most of the time, they are very cool about it. Whenever I call 'em up, they drop whatever they're doin', whatever they're doin', and come to me. A couple of times, girls stopped screwing their boyfriends when I gave 'em a ring. They understand that this kind of quality and quantity is in limited supply. . . .

Let's be honest—sex is what everyone is basically interested in. Great sex with great-looking, great fucks. There are only so many to go around. . . .

I am one.

Sometimes I feel sorry for other people. *(Adjusts his crotch)* Sometimes I feel guilty. It's like I'm living in a color movie, everybody else is living in black and white. But then I think, someone has to live out the dream. Somebody's got to have it all. Might as well be me.

STAG

(A man wearing a T-shirt with sleeves rolled stands poised in the middle of the stage, a beer in one hand, an imaginary football in the other. He's about to throw the ball.)

Terry! Terry! Go out for a long one! Go back! Go back! Go way back! *(Throws the ball)* Hey, watch out for the truck, man, watch out for the—oh . . . shhhhh . . . I told you to watch out for the truck! . . . Hey, I can't help it if you're uncoordinated. . . .

Yo, Terry, Terry, Terry, Terry, if you're goin' to the store to get bandages, get me a pack of cigarettes, please? Winston, hard pack . . . *(He contorts his posture.)* Come on, man, *pleeeeeeasssse!* . . . Thank you.

(He sips from his beer and walks away from the audience toward upstage right, then notices

someone behind him downstage left. He spins and gives the high five.)

Hey, Joey, my man, that pot was great last night, man—you got to get us some more! Yeah, we smoked it all up . . . half-pound only goes so far. . . .

Aaah, the party was great, it was great! You shoulda been there! Me and Frankie, we goes down the corner, we grabs Louie, we kidnaps him. We brings him up to the apartment. We got five cases of beer, three cases of champagne, four bottles of Jack Daniel's, an ounce of blow, and the half-pound of pot. For the three of us, right?

Louie looks around, he goes, "What's all this?" I says, " 'What's all this?'! You're gettin' married tomorrow, man—this is your surprise stag party!"

Louie's lookin' around . . . he goes, "I gotta be at the church by ten o'clock—I can't get too wasted." And Frankie—Frankie's so funny, man, he's cutting lines on the counter, he's cutting lines and he goes, "Don't worry, man, we won't get you *too* wasted."

(Laughs a long, horsey laugh)

Then Frankie—Frankie's so cool, man, he just goes like this . . . *(Snaps his fingers)* The bedroom door opens up and these three beautiful babes come waltzing out of the bedroom wearing bikinis. . . . *(Laughs)* You shoulda seen Louie's face. He looked like he was gonna cry! . . . Yeah, yeah, they're friends of Frankie's—he told 'em if they hung out for the night he'd introduce 'em to Bruce Springsteen. I didn't even know he *knew* Bruce Springsteen. *(Pause)* Oh, he doesn't? Oh . . . So anyways . . .

So we start partying, man . . . champagne, cocaine. . . . Frankie gets out these porno tapes, to warm up the ladies? The nice ones, man—the kind with, like, stories in 'em? One of 'em was so funny, man. How'd it go? Oh, yeah . . . There's this girl, right? And, uh, this chick, she's in her house, ironing her clothes, and there's a knock on the door and the guy goes, "It's the milkman—I have something for you!" Right? And he comes in . . . I don't think it was a real milkman . . . and they start screwing right on the ironing board. Very sensuous, very nicely done. . . .

So then he leaves and there's another knock on the door. And she goes, "Who is it?" and the guy outside goes, "It's—" wait a minute . . . oh, yeah—"It's UPS, I have something for you!" And this guy comes in and he's holding this package like this *(indicates carrying a heavy box)* and she opens it up and *his dick's inside!* Joe, what a riot! I never woulda guessed it in a million years. Huh? There was a hole in the box! And they do it. . . . Then he leaves . . . takes his dick with him. . . . And there's another knock on the door . . . and she says, "Who is it?" And . . . there's no answer.

So she goes over to look out the door—there's nobody there! She opens the door—there's nobody there! She looks down, Joey—there's a *dog* out there! The dog comes trotting in . . . starts licking her feet, licking her legs . . . I can't watch it. . . .

I mean, what am I gonna tell the priest in confession? "Oh, yeah, I was watchin' dog porno tapes." "That's fifteen million Hail Marys, twenty million Our Fathers. . . ."

Hey, man, I don't got the time!

But listen, Joe . . . the girl I'm sittin' with? She's watchin' the whole thing! Oh, yeah, man . . . she's watchin' it. I turns to her, I says, "This stuff turn you on?" She says, "Sure—why not?" Like it's the most normal thing in the world. The rest of the night, man, I'm like checking myself out for fleas!

Great party, man—we had food. I got the food together. You know how you always run out of potato chips? I bought fifty bags of potato chips. The ripple kind, the good kind? Clam dip . . . from the 7-Eleven. . . . We spared no expense.

I'm sittin' there on the couch, man, and I'm thinkin' to myself, "This is the best party I ever been to, man. I'm doing everything I love to do in the whole world!" I got a beautiful girl sitting next to me . . . I'm watchin' TV . . . I'm eating clam dip . . . with a rippled potato chip! I'm smoking joints, I'm snortin' coke, I'm tossin' shots of Jack Daniel's and I'm chasin' 'em with glasses of champagne! I'm thinking to myself, "This is civilized!"

It doesn't get any better than that, man. What more could you want?

And all of a sudden I got depressed, man. You know why? Because I looked over and I saw Louie on the couch and I thought to myself, "He's never gonna have it like this again for the rest of his life." Really, man—think about it. Guys get married and they never have any fun anymore. Might as well shoot 'em in the head and bury 'em. . . . No, come on, Joey—I'm gonna call up Louie six months from now and you know what he's gonna say? I'm gonna call him up and say, "Louie, come on, let's go out, let's play some pool or something." And he's gonna say, "No, I can't . . . I gotta go up to the mall with my wife, look for towels and sheets." Guy's had one towel, one sheet for twenty-five years, now he needs new towels and sheets. . . . Who puts those ideas in a guy's head? You know who! *(Sips beer)* You know fucking who!

(Pause)

So me and Frankie, we're getting wasted. Playing all the old party games—you know: who can snort the most coke, who can make his nose bleed first, who can toss the most shots, who can see double first. . . . Getting totally hammered.

You know when you're like *(indicates)* this close to puking, but you don't puke? We were *there,* man— we were there all fucking night. Just sitting there feeling the brain cells die . . . "Oh, there goes the right side of my brain! *I'm a moron!" (Laughs)*

It was nice, man. Blacked out three times! Woke up, Louie's over with this babe we hooked him up with, this Angela, he's kissing her, he's got his tongue in her ear, his hand up her shirt. . . . Next thing we know, he's going in the bedroom with her. . . . Hey, okay with me—he's not married yet, he's normal, he's got hormones. Go in the bedroom.

So I'm hungry, so I goes into the kitchen. I always get really hungry whenever I'm doing Quaaludes, so I'm frying up these steaks. *(Mimes frying the steaks)* Joey, the whole trick to frying up steaks when you're on 'Ludes is keeping your face outa the frying pan. *(Mimes nodding into the frying pan)* "Whoooooa! Keep burnin' my nose!"

Five minutes goes by . . . Angela comes tearing out of the bedroom, she says, "You guys gotta do something about your friend in there." "What? What?!"

Me and Frankie go running into the bedroom. . . . Louie's sitting in the middle of the bedroom floor, shit-faced, crying his eyes out. No, Joey—really crying. He's sitting there going: "I changed my mind . . . I changed my mind . . . I don't want to get married anymore." I says, "Louie, Louie, you gotta get married, they already hired the hall. . . . You gotta get married, Louie—ya grandmother made lasagne for four hundred people!"

"I don't care! I don't care! I'm in love with *her!*" *(Points)*

He's in love with this Angela! Great! I'm trying to figure this thing out, I'm getting one of those brain tumor headaches . . . all of a sudden, I smell my steaks burning! We runs into the kitchen, and the kitchen, Joe, the kitchen was all like . . . fire . . . all different kinds of fire, burning everything up. So we're taking, like, champagne, we're pouring that on it, we're throwin' beer on it. Frankie goes and gets the TV set, throws that on it. . . .

We finally get the fire out, right? The place stinks, it smells. . . . Steaks stuck to the wall with clam dip . . . place is wrecked. . . . Frankie goes, he goes *(laughing),* "Fuck the fuckin' party, man, the fuckin' party's fucked."

How does he think up those lines, man? He's funny—he should be on TV. . . .

I says, "Wait a minute—apartment's finished, but the party's not finished! Let's go somewhere, have a nice sit-down dinner, have our party there." . . . So anyways, make a long story short, we decide to go down to the new McDonald's.

So we walks into the McDonald's, first thing I see, four Hell's Angels sitting over there having something to eat. Fine, great. We sit over here. . . . The girls are fooling around—you know the way girls get when they're drunk—they get silly. Louie, he's not eatin', he's in love with Angela, he's never gonna eat again for the rest of his life. Frankie, he's not eatin' 'cause every time he gets near Hell's Angels, that scar next to his eye starts to throb.

Me, I'm eatin'. I'm in a McDonald's, I'm gonna eat, I'm not gonna miss the opportunity.

So one of the girls, she takes my ketchup thing—you know, those things of ketchup, whatever you call 'em, ketchup bag—and she squeezes it, and the ketchup goes way up in the air, comes down, goes all over Frankie's shirt. She starts laughin' like this is the funniest thing she ever saw in her whole life. Right? Now all the girls, they start going hysterical.

The Hell's Angels, they see what happened, they start laughin', the manager of the McDonald's, he starts laughin', everybody who works there, they're all laughing. People out in the parking lot, they're laugh-

in'. Everybody in the whole world is laughing at
Frankie. Great, let's make an atom bomb while we're
at it.

I goes over to Frankie, I says, "Frankie, let's go out
and get some fresh air?" He says, "In a minute." I says,
"Frankie, there's four of them, there's three of us, let's
get out of here now." He says, "In a minute."

Frankie stands up, he walks over to the biggest
Hell's Angel, guy isn't even a human being, he's just
this side of a mountain, sitting there.

Guy's got a shaved head, a tattoo of like Satan or
Jesus or some fuck on his forehead, big bushy beard,
ring through his nose. Guy's just sitting there *(imitates
the Angel)*, "Rah-blah-blah."

Frankie goes up to him like this: "Yo, Chief
. . . you lose this?" And he's got one of those like
ketchup things in his hand? He just goes *splllllt,
frlllllllt . . .* right in the guy's face!

*(He acts all of this out, laughing as he tells the
story.)*

Before the guy can even shake his head,
Frankie's like *BANG! BANG! BANG!* right in the
guy's face, kickin' his ass. Fortunately I thought
ahead—I picked up one of those Ronald fucking Mc-
Donald trash cans, I toss it into the teeth of the guy

sitting next to him. So I'm standing there crunching this guy's head, Louie comes over, he's good for nothing, falls on a guy.

The girls, they're throwing french fries, hamburgers. The manager of the McDonald's, he comes running out with a fire extinguisher, sticks it in my ear, turns it on! Like I started it or something! What a rush! Frankie, he jumps over the counter, runs in the back, gets a big potful of that hot french-fry grease, throws it all over these guys. . . .

Me, Frankie, and Louie, we go running out to my car . . . Frankie jumps in, tries to start my car, trying to start the car, car won't start, as usual—gotta get a new starter. I'm sitting there, I'm praying. . . . Louie's in the backseat, he's got the door wide open, hanging out the door, he's goin', "*Angela! ANGELA!*" I says, "Louie, get inside the car, lock the door, come on!"

And that guy, that inhuman mountain guy? Like nothing even happened to him, Joey. He just stands up, starts walkin' right at us in the car *(mimes a Franken-stein-style walk)*—right through the plate-glass window of the McDonald's, man! Boom!

We're just about to take off, the guy reaches out, grabs Louie's leg, Louie grabs me around the neck, Frankie hits the gas, we're pulling this whale all over the parkin' lot. Frankie's trying to scrape the guy off on trash cans, the curb, over those little McDonald bushes they got everywhere. Nothing's workin'. I'm going, "Louie, Louie, hit the guy, kick him, do something!" And Louie—I don't know if he did it on purpose or what—he just turns around, pukes all over the guy's face. . . . *(Laughs)* He let go off him *then,* man!

Louie passes out into the backseat of the car—we slam the door shut, take off like a bat outa hell!

(Laughing, really enjoying himself)

It was fuckin' great, man!

(Catches his breath)

But you know what was really great, man? What was like the icing on the gravy?

We're driving, we're like five miles away, the action's behind us. We're not even going that fast—maybe seventy, seventy-five. And I turns to Frankie and I says, "Frankie, why'd you start all that shit, man? I mean, we coulda gotten killed back there!" And you know what he says, Joey? He doesn't even look at me—he just keeps drivin' and he goes, "Sometimes you gotta spit in the devil's eye . . . just to make sure you're alive."

(Slow smile)

Think about that. Hit my brain like a rock. I'm sitting there and I looks at Louie passed out in the backseat, dreamin' about towels and sheets . . . I looks at Frankie drivin' the car, smokin' a joint, a beer between his legs, the music's blastin', and I thinks to myself, "Yeah, man, yeah—this guy knows what he's talking about. He's never gonna sell out. He's gonna live until the day he dies." *(Raises his fist)* Rock on, man, no surrender!

We drove all the way out to the beach, man . . . we made a little fire on the beach and we just stayed up all night smokin' joints. Smoked up that whole half-pound of pot, man. Didn't even talk. I thought about what he said all night, man. It was heavy.

Watched the sun come up. And I thought about all the water in the ocean. There's a lot of water out there. And that water's just little drops. And I'm like a little drop of water in the world. So I might as well party, man. Might as well party. *(Laughs)* Sun comes up and Louie wakes up, stumbles down to the beach. He goes: "I gotta be at the church at ten o'clock."

He's got puke all over him, he wants to go to church!

So we throw Louie in the backseat of the car, we start driving to the church, run outa gas a mile down the road. . . . Huh? Naw, we got there, we got there. A little late . . . around twelve-thirty. . . .

Yeah, they gotta postpone it to next Saturday. Big deal. It's okay. Louie's okay. . . . Louie's grandmother got one of those little heart attacks.

But listen, Joey—next week, Friday night, we're gonna have another surprise stag party for Louie. Don't tell nobody. . . .

Listen, Joey—one thing. *(He turns and pees against the back wall, then turns to face the audience, zips up.)* . . . If you're gonna come . . . no girls. . . . They cause too much trouble. . . .

BOTTLEMAN

(A man talks quickly, nervously, rarely looking at the audience. He constantly hitches his pants and pats his hair. His overcheerful manner covers his fear. He's making conversation with an imaginary listener.

He begins by talking to the wall.)

I don't like to complain. I'm not a complaining kind of guy, I'm a happy kind of guy—runs in my family, happiness. Never been sick in my life. Not one day. Unless you count broken bones, which I don't. But I like to stay positive. Stay on the sunny side of the street. You give me a pack of cigarettes, egg salad sandwich, cup of coffee, a newspaper, someplace to sit down, and I'm happy—I'm happy.

(Turns, paces, then stops.)

I don't even need the cigarettes. I should quit anyway. It's a dirty habit. Unhealthy. Expensive. Of course you can always find cigarettes. People always have cigarettes—they'll give 'em to you. Food's another subject altogether. People aren't exactly walking around with an egg salad sandwich in their pocket—unless they're crazy! And you figure, egg salad sandwich's gonna run you maybe seventy-eighty bottles. I'm findin' maybe fifty bottles a day—you're talking a shortfall of about twenty bottles . . . or cans . . . bottles or cans, it doesn't make much difference.

(Now another direction, paces, stops.)

Back in the old days, I used to weigh a lot more than I do now. Used to be on a diet all the time. Always trying to lose weight. I don't have that problem anymore. I'm on the egg salad sandwich diet now. One egg salad sandwich every two days . . . you lose weight like crazy. The fat just flies off . . . and it stays off. I'm gonna patent it. Get a copyright and put an ad in the newspaper. Make a little money.

See, newspapers—newspapers, you can get. You can always find a newspaper, people just leave 'em around. And I read 'em. I wanna know about the world.

*(His pacing has him facing completely upstage,
his back to the audience.)*

It's important to stay informed. I read about a
train in Japan goes three hundred miles an hour, gets
you there in no time. They got hotels for cockroaches
now, hotels for mice. I stay away from hotels. Too
much money—who's got that kinda money? Ten
bucks a night, forget it. You figure that's two hundred
bottles—bottles or cans—and that's not in my bud-
get.

*(Now he's facing the audience, talking to the
audience in a detached way.)*

But it's not a problem. You can always find someplace—there's always someplace to stay. You wedge
yourself in someplace. The real problem is the con-
crete. The stone. They make everything out of rocks
and cement! Too hard. What ever happened to wood?
Used to be all the buildings were made out of wood.
Used to make benches outa wood. But no more. Because they make wood outa trees, and trees, they don't
got them no more.

I saw this tree . . . there was this tree, beautiful

tree . . . they dug a hole and put it in the sidewalk.
Every day I come to say hello. And this guy was back-
ing up his truck. The truck was making that beep
sound—*beep-beep-beep-beep*—right over the tree,
'cause, see, the tree can't hear that. See? That was it
for the tree. That was it. What are you gonna do? It's
just in the nature of a tree that if you run 'em over
they die. They're not like people—they can't take the
abuse.

Take a tree, replace it with a metal pole, then
there's no problem. Truck hits the pole, that's it. But
you lose the leaves. You lose the leaves and the twigs.
You lose the wood. Wood is good.

(Paces, suddenly:)

Dogs like wood. I know—I used to have a dog.
Walked him every day. I used to say *(miming walking
the dog):* "Come on! Come on! . . . Who takes care of
you? Who takes care of you? *I* take care of you. . . .
Who's gonna take care of *me* in my old age? Who's
gonna take care of me?" That's what I used to ask
him. . . .

He ran away. But that's okay—they gotta eat too,
the little ones. Everybody's gotta eat, sooner or later.
It's human nature. It's human nature. I like to eat. I
like to eat. Kind of a habit of mine, food.

(He holds an imaginary sandwich before his face.)

Nice egg salad sandwich. Cup a coffee . . . Cream. Sugar.

I'm cutting down on the coffee. I don't drink much coffee these days. Sixty cents a cup. Where did they come up with that figure, that's the question I want to ask. Should be ten cents! But they got ya, see, they got ya. 'Cause they got the beans. They got the beans. You got no choice. They got a cartel. This OPEC.

But I don't need coffee. I don't need the coffee. People drink coffee to stay awake—I don't need to stay awake. I'm awake, I'm awake. When I'm asleep I'm awake. You gotta keep your eyes open when you're sleeping, 'cause you find a place to lie down and you don't keep your eyes open and a guy comes back with a baseball bat and that's it—*bang bang,* you're dead!

No more coffee, no more cigarettes—that's it!

See, these guys on the street, they like to fight. I don't got that luxury. I'm on my second set of teeth, I'm missing a kneecap, I can't hear in one ear. I'm like the bionic man without the hardware. I'm no Cassius Clay. I'm no Cassius Clay.

(Pause)

But I stay on the sunny side of the street. I stay on the sunny side of the street. A guy once told me, "Life is like a half a glass of water . . . half a glass of water . . ."

(He loses his train of thought; his hand is shaking, holding the imaginary glass.)

You got a half a glass a water. . . . "And . . . uh . . . you should drink the water," that's what he said. . . .

(Sheepish—he didn't get the saying right—he turns away, then laughs at himself.)

No, that isn't what he said. . . . He said . . . he said . . . "Half a glass of water is better than no water at all!" That's it. "Half a glass of water is better than no water. . . ."

(Full of energy again)

I look at it this way—I could be living in Ethiopia. Those poor people got it terrible. They got nothing to eat. Starving all the time. They just sit in the sand all day long. . . . It's too sunny, too many flies . . . it's not

for me. It's not my bag. I prefer it here . . . it's better
here.

(Lost in thought, convincing himself)

It's good here, it's good. It's good. Thank God!

*(Pause. He's just standing, staring at the
ground.*
*He snaps out of it—sunny, cheerful again,
he addresses the audience.)*

Well, I gotta get going, got to get to work. You
know what they say: "The early bird catches the can!"
Or bottles . . . bottles or cans, it don't make no
difference. . . .

(He walks off upstage, still talking.)

It don't make no difference at all. . . .

CANDY

(The sound of a push-button phone being dialed; then a recorded sexy voice is heard:)

Hi, I'm Candy. I'm glad you called. I was just about to take a really, really erotic bath, and I thought, "Wouldn't it be nice if a really, really horny guy called up so I could tell him all about it?" . . . I can't think of anything sexier than having a really, really horny guy listening to my deepest and most . . . intimate . . . erotic fantasies. . . . It gets me *sooooo* excited, I feel all tingly and pink, it makes me just want to pull off all my clothes and dance around the room listening to some really, really *hard* rock. Ooooooh, I get goose bumps just thinking about it! Sometimes when I'm really, really horny I have to call just two or three of my best girlfriends up and they come over and we just take all our clothes off and rub olive oil all over our bodies and then do really really vigorous aerobics. Ohhhh, my bathtub's all filled up, and I'm ready to jump in and scrub myself all over. If you want to "come" along, call me back and press two on your touch-tone phone for more erotic adventures. I can't wait.

ROCK LAW

(Lights up on a man sitting in an office chair, rolling across the stage. He jumps out of the chair, shouting into a hand-held phone. He paces, he contorts his body, as he yells into the phone.)

Frank, Frank, Frank . . . what did he say? He's gonna sue me? He's gonna sue me? Did you tell him who he's messing with here, Frank? Did you tell him who he's *fucking* with here, Frank? He's fucking with *God,* Frank—did you tell him that? Did you tell him what God *does* when he gets fucked with, Frank? Ever hear of Sodom and Gomorrah, Frank? That's what I'm gonna do to his *face!*

No, no, no, no, no, Frank—I don't want to hear it. Sue me? Sue me? I'm gonna blow him away, Frank, I'm gonna peel his skin off, I'm gonna chew his bones,

I'm gonna drink his blood, I'm gonna *eat his children*, Frank!

And I'm gonna enjoy myself—you wanna know why? Because he's a schmuck, a schlemiel, and shithead for fucking with me, that's why! He should know better! . . .

No, no, no, Frank—I'm not listening to another word! *(Sings loudly: La-la-la-la, la-la-la-la!)* Sue me? *Sue me?* Call him back right now and tell him . . . tell him . . . *Wait*—don't call him back, don't call him. . . . Call his children, call his children and tell them to *get ready to be eaten!* Good-bye, Frank!

(He strides over to a small table stage left and yells into an intercom.)

DIANE! DIANE! Who's on line one? . . . My wife? Put her on hold . . . What's for lunch? I'm starving to death. . . . I don't care, anything. . . . I don't care, Diane, anything—*I am starving to death! (Pause)* No, I don't want that! *(Pause)* No, I don't want that, either . . . no monkfish . . . no monkfish, no arugula, no sun-dried tomatoes, no whole-wheat tortellini. . . . I want *food*, Diane—you know what I mean when I say "food"? Diane, unlike you I am a human being, I need food, I need coffee—please get me some.

. . . Call Jeff Cavanaugh, put him on line two—call Dave Simpson, put him on line three . . . *thank you!*

(Taps a button on his hand-held phone, becomes cordial and familiar)

Hi, honey. . . . I know! I tell her time and time again, "Don't put my wife on hold," she puts you on hold. I'm sorry. What did you do today? . . . That's nice—how much did that cost? . . . No, no, no! Spend the money—that's what it's there for. . . . That's what it's there for. . . . *(Rubs his forehead)*

How's Jeremy? . . . Why did he do that? No, no—why did he bite the kid, Sonia? . . . I told him to? I did not tell him to bite anybody. . . . Sonia, I did not tell him— . . . Don't tell me what I tell him. . . . I told him— . . . Can I talk, please? I told him, "The next time a little boy does something to you, do twice as much back to him," that's what I told him. I don't care what his therapist says! I don't care what his therapist says—his therapist is a co-dependent dysfunctional fraud! . . . No, no, wait—you know what I'm going to tell Jeremy? I'm gonna say, "Jeremy, bite your therapist!" Let him work on that for a while.

What else? . . . How did she do that? How did she get it in the microwave, Sonia? . . . No, wait, that's what?—three microwave ovens in two years? . . . We have to buy another microwave now? . . . No, no, I just want to say something: If you hired people who came from a country where they had electricity, we wouldn't have this problem. . . . Well, you gotta tell her. . . . What do you mean, "She'll quit"? . . . She won't quit—she's got it great. She spends all day in a luxury New York apartment! I spend all day in this office killing myself so she can spend all day in my luxury New York apartment! She spends more time there than I do!

I AM NOT SHOUTING! *(Lowers his voice)* I am not . . . this is not shouting. . . . Am I shouting? Now wait a minute, am I shouting? Is this shouting? This is not shouting—this is discussing. We are discussing . . . we are having a discussion.

(Patronizing) Well, obviously you're too agitated to have a normal conversation right now, so why don't we wait until I get home. . . . I'm gonna be a little late tonight. . . . Around nine. . . .

I have a lot of work to do! Sonia, do you think I like slaving and sweating here all hours of the night and day so that you and Jeremy can be safe and free? Do you?

It hasn't been two weeks . . . It hasn't been two weeks, we just did it the other—

Okay, okay . . . we'll have sex tomorrow night, all right? . . . I won't forget—I'll put it in my book!

Listen, honey, I've been working very hard. Next month, we'll go down to Saint Bart's, we'll get a place by the beach, we'll make love every day on the beach. . . .

You won't get sand in your crotch! Look, I gotta get off, I got twenty people on hold. . . .

Huh? . . . No, don't color your hair—no, don't cut your hair, either! Nothing with your hair. . . . Don't start with the hair blackmail now. . . . No henna, nothing! I want you to look the same when I get home tonight as you did when I left this morning, that's what I want. . . . I gotta get off. . . .

Give Jeremy a kiss good night for me, okay? Say hi to your mother for me, too. . . . Okay, all right. . . . What?! . . . Orange juice. Fine. Okay. . . . I love you too . . . I'll be home around ten-thirty. . . . Bye!

(Goes over to intercom)

Diane, what are you doing in there, *growing the food?!* Come on! I feel like a poster child for Ethiopian relief. My ribs are sticking out, flies are crawling all over me, I'm gonna be dead in five minutes—come on!

(Punches a button on his phone, starts to speak, then relaxes into chair stage right and carries on a very casual conversation)

Jeff? Hey, man, how they hanging? . . . Not bad, not bad. . . . Yeah, I finished that deal yesterday. . . . No, I made twenty grand—chump change. Listen to this, man—this morning I cut a deal I made seventy-five grand. You know what they say: "A hundred grand here, a hundred grand there—pretty soon you're talking real money." . . .

I don't know—maybe I'll buy a Porsche for the country house, park it in front of the tennis court, piss off my neighbors. Not even drive it, just leave it there all the time. . . . Huh? No, I can't drive it—I don't drive a stick. . . . That's an idea—Range Rover, they're good. Very ecological, right? Maybe I'll get one of those.

Naw, I can't, not tonight. I'm doin' something. . . . *Who* am I doin'? I'm not telling you. Jeff, I tell you, you're gonna tell Nadine and she'll tell Sonia. . . . Very beautiful. . . . Better. . . . Better than her. . . . Better than her. . . . Yeah, she has breasts—yeah, she has legs, she has arms, she has a head. I got the whole package. Jeff, the closest you ever came to a girl this beautiful is that time you bought the scratch-and-sniff picture of Vanna White . . . ha-ha . . . And get this, she's an artist. She's very, very sensitive. She picked me up in a bar— how could I say no?

Jeff, unlike you, I am still committed to my sixties idealism. I'm still committed to experience and exploration. . . . Unfortunately, you gave up the struggle a long time ago; but for me, it's a matter of principle.

Why don't we get together tomorrow night, play some handball, have a couple of pops over at my club? . . . No, *my* club, my club, Jeff. My club is nicer than your club—it's safer, it's cleaner, it's more exclusive. . . .

(Stands up)

Okay? I gotta get off the phone, I have a lot of work to do, unlike you. . . . Thank you . . . thank you. I am a genius. I am the best. No one can get close to me. I'll let *you* get close to me, Jeff, you can blow me. . . . Bye!

(Pushes more buttons on his phone and keeps talking, with a more aggressive, impatient tone, pacing once again)

Dave, Dave, can I say just one thing here? I agree with you one hundred and fifty percent! . . . No, no, Dave, the man is a wonderful human being, he's a mensch, he's a lovely person. . . . I love him, I felt terrible having to let him go. . . .

Yes, I understand that, I know he's fifty-eight

years old. . . . I know he's gonna lose his pension. . . . I understand that, but Dave, Dave, Dave, Dave! . . .

There's two sides to this argument—don't forget the human side of the equation! . . .

Now, when I first came to work at this company, this man was like a father to me—he's like my own father, this guy. I love him—we're like blood relatives. . . . It broke my heart to *have to have to fire him, Dave!* . . .

Yes, yes, yes . . . I know he's going in for major surgery next week—that's not my problem, I'm not his doctor, Dave, I'm his boss.

No . . . no . . . no . . . but—but—but—but Dave! Dave! Now you've been talking for five minutes straight, can I get a word in edgewise here? The guy . . . the guy is not performing anymore. He's not hustling anymore. He's easy listening and this place is rock and roll! I need heavy metal here, Dave—I need production—I need performance!

Yes, but Dave, Dave, Dave!

Let me make it a little clearer for you: You like your Mercedes station wagon? You like your country house? You like your swimming pool? You like skiing in Aspen? You like long lunches, your car phone, that horsey school you send your daughter to? What pays for those things, Dave? Now, wait—what do you think pays for those things?

Profits, that's what—say "profits," Dave! Say "profits" . . . I just want to hear you say it . . . Say it! Thank you. . . .

Now, now, now, Dave, when the profit ax comes down, anybody's head can roll. I could lose my job tomorrow, you could lose your job tomorrow. You could lose your job today, you could lose your job in the next five minutes if we keep up this stupid conversation. Because, to tell you the truth, Dave, I want to get rid of the guy even more now, because now he's wasting *your* time as well as mine. You're wasting your time, I'm wasting my time, all these people in this company are wasting their time around here, and I have to say to myself, "What's the point?" What's the point, Dave—what's the point. What is your fucking goddamn point!? WILL YOU TELL ME WHAT YOUR FUCKING GODDAMN POINT IS, PLEASE?

Dave? . . .

You're not sure? Well, let me ask you this: Are you happy working for this company? . . . No, I mean, are you happy working for this company? . . . You are? Good, because I just want you to be happy . . . so get back to work.

(Suddenly laughs)

Okay. . . . All right. . . . No, no—no hard feelings. We've all been working hard. . . . Okay. . . . All right, I understand. . . . Call anytime. . . . Say hi to Judy for me. . . . Janet? . . . Say hi to Janet. . . . Okay . . . All right. . . . Take care.

(He switches off, then yells into the intercom.)

DIANE, LET ME MAKE IT EASY FOR YOU: TAKE YOUR HAND, PUT IT IN THE MICRO-WAVE, GRILL IT, BRING IT IN TO ME!
WHO'S ON LINE FOUR? . . .
I GOT IT.

(Pushes more buttons on his phone; then, very relaxed, sultry:)

Hi . . .
Nothing . . . I'm making money—what else do I do? . . . I'm working very hard . . . now that you called it's getting harder and harder. . . . Um-hmmmm. . . .

(Sits in his chair)

You being a good girl? . . . Oh, yeah? What are you doing? . . . Making a sculpture, that's interesting. What kind of sculpture? . . . You made a sculpture of a horse and you wrote the word "horse" all over it? That's very conceptual, Yvette. . . .

(He checks his watch, stifles a yawn.)

What do you mean, I sound bored? Of course I'm not bored, I love talking about your art! I was just telling someone ten minutes ago what a wonderful art you have. . . . Yvette, Yvette, can I just say something? . . . No, can I say something?

If you were ninety-five years old and you were in a wheelchair, I would still love you, and you want to know why? Because I love your art, that's why. . . . Of course I mean it, of course I mean it—and when you say these mean things to me I get all angry and confused . . . and . . . and I feel like coming over there and . . . giving you a good spanking!

(The serious look on his face melts into pleasure as he listens to what she's going to do to him.*)*

Ooohhh . . . that would hurt! All over my body! And then what are you going to do? . . . The whole

thing!? The phone is heating up, Yvette—stop it!
. . . No, not that! Anything but that *(laughs)* . . .

What did I do to deserve all this attention? I am a pretty nice guy, aren't I? . . .

Um-hmm . . . I love you too. I love you too. . . . Of course I mean it. Yvette, when I say I love you, I mean I love you. No one else in the whole world knows what love means the way that I know what love means when I say from me to you "I love you." No one was ever loved before the way that I love when I love you. Because my life would have no meaning if I didn't love you.

(Through all of the above, he has become fascinated with a smudge of dirt on his shoe. He's been picking at it as he speaks, and now is totally engrossed in the smudge, but he keeps talking without missing a beat.)

Of course I mean it, of course I mean it. Would I lie to you? . . .

(Checks his watch)

Listen, Yvette, the boss just walked in—I gotta get off. . . . When am I going to see you? . . . Around six? At the loft? Okay . . . I will. . . . Keep making those sculptures. . . . Ciao to you too.

(He blows her a noisy kiss over the phone, switches off, and lurches at the intercom.)

Diane, cut the food, cut the coffee. Send in the Maalox, the shoeshine boy, and hold my calls. Thank you!

(Blackout to silhouette)

X-BLOW

(A man in silhouette declaims to a rap beat:)

I'm a child of nature, born to lose—
people call me "Poison" but that's no
    news.
When I wake up in the morning, I see
    what I see,
I look into the mirror, what I see is me:
A player, a winner, an unrepentant
    sinner—
if you mess with me, I'll eat you for
    dinner.
There are those that rule and those that
    serve,
I'm the boss, baby, 'cause I got the nerve
to take what I want, take what I need,
cut you first, sucker, and make you bleed.

'Cause life's a bitch, that I know.
Don't misunderstand me or then you'll go
to your grave in a rocket, nothing in your
    pocket,
if you got a gun, you better not cock it,
'cause then you'll die, that I know,
what's left of you away will blow
and you will spend eternity
praying to God you never met me!
Huh-huh-huh-huh-huh!

*(He steps into the light and addresses the
audience, telling the story in a friendly manner.)*

Sucker dissed me, man, he dissed me! I had no
choice. He showed me his gun, so I walked up to him,
I stuck my screwdriver into his stomach, and I ran it
right true his heart. He looked surprised, man. Skinny
kid like me, killing him like dat. Hah. Didn't even
bleed.

Felt good, man, felt better than gettin' laid on a
sunny day. And I like to feel good. Feeling good makes
me feel good. Don't need no sucker drugs to feel good.

'Fore they locked me up I used to get up every
morning and I had me two problems: how to find
money, how to spend it. All the rest was gravy. Like the
man says, "Don't worry, be happy."

That was the Reagan years, and the Reagan years is over, man, and I miss 'em! Ronnie Reagan, he was my main man. He had that cowboys-and-Indians shit down. Now he's out in L.A. sitting on a horse and we're sitting in the shit he left behind. But it's okay he's gone. New man's in charge! *Batman!* Batman is my man!

Gonna be beaming around like Kirk and Scotty, like the Jetsons, man! Just beaming around, beaming around. Jump into my Batmobile, get behind some smoked bulletproof windshield, stick in the CD, flip the dial to ten, rock the engine, burn the brakes. . . . Man, that's living . . . you can smoke that shit!

You only live once, you gotta grab that gusto shit.

My best friend in school went to work at McDonald's—worked hard too! First he 'came 'sistant manager, then he 'came manager. Guess he figured if he worked hard enough, one day he's gonna be president of McDonald's. Making four-fifty a week, had it nice, man. Had himself a duplex rental 'partment and a Ford Escort.

One Friday night some homeboys came in with a .38 special, greased him for the receipts, man. . . . Bang, bang in the back of the head—execution style!

Sucker! He missed the whole point! He's standing on that platform and that train be gone!

See, you wanna play the game, you gotta think

about the big guy, you gotta think about God! God made man same as hisself. You wanna learn how to live, live like God! Check the big guy out!

God, man, he gets up every morning, he don't smoke no crack, he don't shoot no dope. God don't flip no burgers. No, man—he gets up and he looks down on the world and he says *(hands on hips)*, "World, what am I gonna do with you today? *(Stretches out his arms)* Lessee, how about this, I will make an earthquake today . . . or how about dis, a tidal wave?

Or, lessee, maybe I'm a little bored, I think I will crack up some trains in India, kill me up some dotheads. . . .

Or maybe I'm feeling a little evil, maybe I jus' burn down an elementree school, fry up some nineyear-olds. . . .

Or maybe I'm feeling real evil, I'll mix up some new disease, sprinkle it all over them homosexual faggots, fuck 'em up, make 'em miserable, make 'em cry and die a slow evil death!

See, God's a player, he likes the action! God likes to rock, he likes to get high. . . . But God don't shoot no dope, he don't shoot no dope—he lets the dopes shoot each other!

Man, I *know* how he feels!

'Fore I was in the joint, used to get me a ten-gauge shotgun, shoot me up some sewer rats. You hit one square, they just vaporize. Like with a ray gun! Makes a nice sound too—BOOM! That must be what it's like to be God, lots of noise and destruction and fun!

See—people, they don't *understand* God. Last summer I was running down the street in my home neighborhood. Typical day for me—guy's chasing me, wants to put a bullet in my head. . . . So I jumps inside of this church, middle of the day . . . and there be this buncha little kids in the church with their teacher. Prayin'. In the middle of the day. Little tiny heads, little tiny butts.

I said, "Yo, teacher, whachoo be doin' in this here church for in the middle of the day?" She says, "Boy, we's in here prayin'—we's prayin' for peace, we's praying against nuclear disarmament."

Hah! I starts laughin'. I says, "Baby, you be prayin' in the wrong place! This here's God's house. You best go pray someplace else. Who you think make all that war shit up in the first place? Who you think make that nuclear bomb up, made up the poison gas and dynamite, rockets and bombs? They's his toys, baby!" I's laughin' so hard, I fell right down on the floor of the church, my gun fell outa my pocket, went off, shot a hole right true the cross on the altar!

See you gotta figure: you wanna run with the big guy, you gotta think big. That's what I do—I think bigger every day. 'Cause God, that's where all the power is. I want to get closer to the power, I want to get more and more spiritual, get closer to God.

That's why next time I gets out, I'm gonna get me some new wheels and an Uzi, man.

Peoples, you gotta wake up, smell the coffee.

(Turns to go)

"What goes around comes around." If you can't dig that shit, you better get out of Gotham City.

(Walks off)

LIVE

(A man walks to the edge of the apron, cigar in hand. He stands erect, chest thrust forward. Gruff, ethnic American accent.)

JIMMY! I'm out in the backyard, here! Come out to the backyard!

(Feels his belly)

Ugghhh . . . every time I have the fried calamari with the hot sauce, I feel like I'm gonna blow up!

So what do you think?

Olympic size, Olympic size! I said to the guy, "I want the best pool you got—gimme the biggest, the best pool you got! I don't care what it cost!"

I got a motto, Jimmy, very simple: "Take care of

the luxuries, the necessities will take care of themselves."

You only live once, Jimmy—you gotta go for the best in this life, you gotta grab all the gusto you can.

I dunno, one hundred grand? It's not important.

It's like when I was buying my BMW . . . I says to myself, I can buy the 750 or I can save a little money, buy a 535. . . . But then I thinks to myself, I buy the 535, I'm in the middle of the highway someplace, 750 passes me, I'm gonna get pissed off! Another eight hundred, nine hundred bucks a month—why waste the aggravation, buy the 750!

You should get yourself a BMW, Jimmy. . . . What do you mean you can't afford it, of course you can afford it, don't give me that crap!

You know what's wrong with people like you, Jimmy?—and I'm just trying to be helpful here— you're full of crap, see? The only thing that's stopping you from having the car of your dreams is fear. You're afraid. You're afraid to have, you're afraid to own, you're afraid to live.

How much are you making now a year? Nineteen grand a year? Twenty-two grand a year? Get yourself a BMW! What are you afraid of?

You gotta live, Jimmy—that's what life is all about. I want to buy something, I buy it! I want to go someplace, I go there!

See this cigar? This is a Havana cigar. Why do I smoke Havana cigars? Because it's the best cigar, that's why. I could smoke something else. I could save myself fifteen bucks a pop, I could smoke something else. Why should I? So somebody else can smoke this cigar? Fuck him, it's my cigar.

It's my cigar—it's my life and I'm living it.

I exercise. Now we got the pool, I come out here every morning, I jump in the pool, I swim a whole lap. Then I go in the house, I have a healthy breakfast. I eat those oat bran muffins. I can't stand 'em, but I eat 'em, they're supposed to be good for you. . . . I have four or five muffins, scrambled eggs, bacon, sausage . . . big pot of black coffee, and I'm alive, Jimmy, I'm alive!

I'm fifty-one years old, I still make love to my wife like it's our wedding night. I know guys ten years younger than me, they don't even know they got a dick! They're in the shower in the morning . . . "La . . . la . . . la, la . . . Oh! What's that?" They think it's a growth sticking out of their body!

(Smokes his cigar, contemplates the horizon)

See that there—you know what that is? That's a gazebo. Guy who sold me the pool, he says you gotta have a gazebo if you're gonna have a swimming pool.

That's the best one they make—cost me five grand. I don't even know what it is.

(Puffs contentedly on his cigar)

See, perfect example of what I'm saying here . . . Vito Schipletti! Never did nothing in his life. He never smoked, he never drank, he never chased skirts, never gambled, never walked when it said "Don't walk!"

You know where he is today with all his money in the bank? He stands in front of the old candy store from nine o'clock in the morning till nine o'clock at night. He lived his life so good, he forgot to live.

What's the point of being alive like him? You might as well be dead!

Jimmy, they tell you cigars take three years off your life. What three years? What three years? Eighty-six to eighty-nine? Who needs 'em! Gimme the cigars!

There are people, Jimmy, all over the world, starving to death, in Africa and Asia, Armenia, they sit around all day starving . . . just sitting in the dirt. Those people, all they got is dreams. They dream, "What would it be like to live in America? What would it be like to have a car, a house, food, a swimming pool. . . . Jimmy, I can't let those people down. . . . I'm here, I'm living it, I might as well enjoy it. . . .

I read in a magazine about a new resort in Hawaii where you can swim with the dolphins. . . . *Bango!* I'm there. They open a new casino down Atlantic City, I'm there the first day it opens. . . . They make a new TV set, ten feet wide, two stories high, I buy it.

'Cause it's my life, Jimmy, it's my life. If I don't live it, who's gonna?

I'm gonna live until the day I die, then I can rest.

(Steps toward the edge of the stage)

You know what you need, Jimmy? You need a nice swim in my new swimming pool. . . . Put on your suit, come on! Snap out of it! *(Bends over the edge of the stage and tests the "water")* The water's not cold—jump in!

DOG CHAMELEON

(A man sits in a chair, talking into a microphone with suppressed anger. He tries to be pleasant.)

Hey, I want to be normal, just like every other guy! Don't leave me out, come on! There's got to be more to life than worrying about the price of cigarettes, getting a job, what's on TV. I know—I know about normalcy. Don't tell me about normalcy!

I want to drive a station wagon with a bunch of kids singing Christmas carols in the backseat. I want to go to the supermarket and compare prices. I want to lose weight while I sleep. I want to buy life insurance. I want to wear pajamas and a bathrobe, sneak into the kitchen in the middle of the night and steal a drumstick out of the refrigerator. Worry about my dog's nutrition. Or maybe just order something from the L. L. Bean catalogue . . . a nice down parka maybe, a flannel shirt . . . something in corduroy!

I know all about normalcy!

I want to yell at my wife when she goes on a spending spree! I want to help my kids with the grades! I want to fertilize my lawn. I want to order my hamburger *my way!* I want to donate money to impoverished minorities!

But all that stuff costs money. Being normal is expensive, you know.

(Short pause)

There was this rat scratching inside my wall the other night. After a while it sounded like it was inside my head. *And I said, "Wait a minute! Wait one minute! I'm white, I'm an American! I'm a male! I should be doing better than this!"*

Ozzie and Harriet didn't have rats in the wall. There were no roaches in the Beaver's room! Even Mister Ed had *heat!* WHAT THE FUCK IS THIS?

The rat kept scratching and I realized something: Times have changed.

It's a race to the death now. Anyone waiting around for the good life to show up is a *fool!* Anyone who thinks that playing fair will get you anywhere is *blind!*

Then I said, "Calm down, calm down, you're getting all excited about nothing. Sure you're poor, you're an artist! You have an artistic sensibility! Artists are supposed to be poor."

And the rat-scratch voice inside my head said, "Fuck that!"

I want to be rich. And I want to be famous. These are normal desires, that should not be thwarted. If you thwart them, if you repress them, you get cancer.

Shit, I want *fame!* Look at *me,* man! Fame is what counts. Fame with money. Any jerk can go to the top of some tower with a scope rifle and start shooting at people. That's shitty fame. I want the good kind. The kind with lots and lots of money. Any slob can win the lottery, it takes *skill* and *brains* to get the fame and the money *at the same time . . .* that's success, man. So everyone looks at you, wherever you go, and they say: "That guy, he did it. He got everybody to look at him, admire him and give him money, their money, at the same time!"

I heard about this guy, he made four hundred

million dollars. Four hundred million dollars! I'd be happy with fifty million. Most people would still think I was a success, even if I wasn't as successful as that guy. I don't care what they think! I wouldn't even tell them how much money I have! I'd just ride around in my stretch limousine, and when I got tired of that I'd go home and I'd have this enormous mansion with fifty rooms. . . . And . . . and I'd have this room with a trench around it full of pit bulls, and I'd have a chair that tilts back and a TV set with remote control and a big bowl of potato chips!

And I'd just watch TV all day and change the channels. Maybe I'd just sit in a large bathtub with lots of bubbles. Smoke a cigar like Al Pacino in *Scarface.* . . . But I wouldn't take drugs or have sex. Too dangerous. Just gimme the money, and the food, and the dark room . . . and the TV set. And a gun—so I can shoot the TV set when somebody I don't like comes on.

I hate people. They get in the way of a good time. Just when everything's getting good, they want something from you!

But I want you all to love *me.* Even though I hate all of you. Just to confirm my deep-seated feeling that you're all scum compared to my beneficence.

Just joking. Just joking. Don't get all excited. Nothing to get excited about. Just love me. Tell me I'm great. And pay me. And then we'll be even. For all the shit you've given me my whole fucking life! I know, I know what you're all thinking. "What a jerk. All he does is talk about himself." Yeah? And what do you do? LISTEN!

I was wronged when I was little. I never really got what I wanted. Now it's time to even the score. Even if I tell you my plans you can't stop me. I'm gonna become so rich and powerful, no one will touch me.

And all those rich fucks who lorded over me, all those muscular jocks who kicked sand in my face, all those big-boobed blondies who laughed at me when I asked them for a date, all those parsimonious paternal patronizing administrators at school and at the unemployment office and at the IRS and the police station . . . you'll all be sorry. You have no idea what I've got in store for you. Hah!

You know what it means to be really, really rich? You walk into a store and the jerk behind the counter gives you some kind of shit like . . . like, I don't know, smirking at you because he thinks you can't afford the most expensive watch in the case. . . . You know the look they give you, they humor you: "Yes, sir, may I help you?"

He doesn't want to help me, he doesn't want to help anybody—he just wants to laugh at me! Won't show me the watch, won't take it out, won't even tell me the price. . . .

Well, when I make it, I'm going to go back to that store and I'm not going to buy one watch, I'm not going to buy ten watches—I'm going to buy the whole store, and then I'm going to fire that patronizing jerk for laughing at me. . . . And then, I'm going to find out where he lives and I'm going to buy his apartment building and I'm going to have him evicted . . . one more pathetic homeless person walking the streets in a state of permanent depression!

Or those big thugs that push into you when you're walking down the street and don't say they're sorry or nothing. Why? Because they think I can't fight back. They think I'm afraid of them. Well, when I make it, I'm gonna get me some bodyguards. They'll walk with me when I'm going down the street. And some fucker pushes into me and I'll just step aside and there's my boy with the sock filled with marbles. Or the straight razor. Or the .38. He won't know what's hit 'im. He'll just end up on the ground, bleeding, looking up at me with glazed eyes, and I'll just lean over and step over 'im and say, "Excuse me."

(Laughs)

You think I should be ashamed of myself? I HAVE NO GUILT! Because I am not a man. I am a dog.

(Barks a long howl)

You know what I find fascinating? Human nature. The nature of human beings . . . what they like, what they don't like, what turns them on, what turns them off. What incredible appetites they have. Night after night they stay glued to their TV sets watching some pinheaded newscaster going on and on about today's grisly murder or vicious rape. They munch on popcorn and suck up TV dinners as they absorb the minutiae pertaining to the day's massive mud slide or exploding chemical plant.

(Mimicking the newscaster)

"Thousands dead and dying! Hundreds blinded!" Munch . . . munch . . . "Carol, get some more salt while you're in the kitchen! . . . Oh, wait, wait, come here, you have to see this—they're completely buried! Come on, you'll miss it, there's a commercial coming on!"

Then, these same people watch shows on educational TV about dolphins, *then* they cry. . . . Then they stay up late to watch some old Christmas movie with Jimmy Stewart standing on a bridge on Christmas Eve; *then* they go berserk!

The next morning, they jump into their sporty compact cars, drink ten cups of coffee, and race each other on the highway while they sing along with some ardent rock singer screaming and yelling about emaciated, dark-skinned, hopeless people turning to dung half a world away.

So they feel so guilty they race home and write out a check for five dollars and mail it to some post-office box in New York City and then they feel so good about themselves they go to bed with each other and they kiss and they lick and they suck each other and they hold each other really really tight, because they really, really care. . . .

(Pause)

I know I'm negative. I know I'm not a nice guy.

I know you all hate me. But I don't care. Because at least I realize I'm a shit, and for that tiny fragment of truth, I respect myself. That's why normalcy is so far out of my reach. Because you have to be blind to be normal. You have to like yourself, and the thought of that is so repellent to me that I'm ecstatic to be in the depressing place that I am!

ARTIST

(A man sits cross-legged in the middle of a pool light, downstage center. He mimes smoking a joint and passing it to an unseen companion.)

It's like if a tree falls in the forest—you know what I'm saying, man? It's like if everybody already knows everything, then nothing means anything. Everything's a cliché.

That's why I stopped making art.

(Takes the joint and tokes)

You know what's wrong with the world today? Why everything's screwed up and you can't do anything about it? Because we don't live in a human world—we live in a machine world.

(Passes the joint)

There's this guy, I can see him from my apartment, down in his apartment across the street. All night long, every night, he lies on his couch, doesn't move for hours on end, his eyes wide open. . . . Now if I didn't know that guy was watching TV, I'd think there was something seriously wrong with him, like he was paralyzed or hypnotized or something. . . .

All night long he lies there, and messages from outer space go into his brain: "Buy a new car," "Use deodorant," "Work harder," "Your dog has bad breath," "Buy a microwave oven." . . . All night long, man, into his brain.

(Takes the joint and tokes)

I mean, what's a microwave oven, man? Everybody's got one, nobody knows what it does, nobody knows how it works, everybody's got one. Why? Why does everybody have a microwave oven?

Because the TV set told 'em to buy it, that's why.

(Tokes and passes)

I'm telling you, man, the government is building this computer, biggest computer they ever built.

Spending billions and billions of dollars. It's a secret project, but I read about it. . . .

When they finish this computer we're all gonna be dead, man. . . . 'Cause they're gonna hook this huge computer up to everybody's TV set. Then they're gonna reverse the TV set so it can see you in your house doing your thing? Computer's gonna watch you, man, and if you do something the computer doesn't like, it's gonna send a message to the TV set. TV set's gonna send a message to the microwave oven, door's gonna pop open, you're gonna be *ashes*, man. . . .

Don't believe me? Go in a store, pick something up, pick anything up, take a look . . . everything's got those little computer lines on 'em now. Everything. What do those little lines mean, man?

Nobody knows. Nobody knows what they say— it's not English, it's computer. All these computers are talking to each other, man, nobody knows what they're saying. It's like we're living in an occupied country, man.

All day and all night long, the computers are talking to each other on the modems and the fax machines and the satellite link-ups. All day and all night. What are they talking about? What are they talking about? I'll tell you what they're talking about. They're talking about you and me . . . how to use us more efficiently. . . .

See, they don't have feelings, man, they're just machines. All they care about is efficiency.

The worst human being who ever lived had feelings, man. Genghis Khan had feelings. Adolf Hitler had feelings. Every once in a while he'd get a little bummed out. Computers never get bummed out, man, never.

(Tokes on the pot, passes it back)

You know how they make bacon? No, I mean, you know how they make bacon? They got these giant meat-packing plants out in Idaho, run by robots and computers. And way down at the bottom of the assembly line they have to have a human being to hold the meat? 'Cause every piece of meat is different. And these twenty-four razor-sharp blades come down, slice through the meat, and that's how you get a slab of bacon.

So some dude comes into work, isn't thinking about what he's doing—maybe he had a fight with his old lady the night before, whatever—sits down at his spot, down come the twenty-four razor-sharp blades, and instead of a hand, he's got a half-pound of sliced and smoked Armour Star.

(Tokes)

Bummer, right?

Happens about once a week. And nobody does anything about it. Nobody cares. Who's to care? Machines run everything now, man.

Every day the machines put more oil in the water, more poison in the air, they chop down more jungles. What do they care? They don't breathe air, they don't drink water.

We do.

(He looks at the joint, considers it for a moment, then swallows it. A strange look comes over his face.)

Stoned, man.

Wish we had some music to listen to. I used to love to listen to rock when I got high. All the great old bands—the Jefferson Airplane, the Stones, the Who.

They're all dead now. . . .

What, those bands touring around? You think that's the Stones, man? You think that's the Who?

Robots, man.

They gotta be robots. Listen to the music. The old bands, what did they sing about? Love, Peace, Anarchy, Freedom, Revolution, Get High. . . . What do the new bands sing about? Fear, Paranoia, Work Harder, Buy a Microwave Oven. . . .

They're just trying to brainwash us, man. They're just part of the system—if they weren't part of the system, you'd never even hear about 'em. All the bands that fought the system—Janis, Jimi, Morrison—they killed 'em all, made it look like accidents. They're all gone now, man, all that's left is the system.

And the system only has one message, man—fear. That's all they tell us all day long, fear. Because we're like little mice in our cages, man, running on our wheels as fast as we can, because we're so afraid.

Every day, get up seven A.M., drink two cups of caffeine, jump in the car, get stuck in traffic, get to work, get yelled at by the boss, make a deadline, drink more caffeine, get back in the car, get stuck in traffic again, get home, pay bills you can't afford, eat your microwave dinner, jump into bed. . . . Oh, wait, wait, I forgot the most important thing—watch a little TV—gotta get those messages in the head!

Get up the next morning, do it over again, get up the next morning, do it over again. Do it over again, do it over again, over again, over again. . . .

They call that being responsible, man. Everybody's scared, man—they're afraid they don't do what they're supposed to do, bang, they're homeless.

That's what the homeless people are, man. They're the warning to all of us, "Stay in your cage, don't rock the boat."

Ever talk to any of those guys on the street, man? Everybody says they're crazy. You live on the street for a while, see what kind of ideas *you* come up with. You don't go crazy, man—you start to see the truth. You start seeing the truth, you start telling the truth, you start talking about the way things really are.

That's why they keep those guys out on the street, man. The system's afraid of them. Afraid of their freedom. Freedom is the opposite of responsibility. Freedom is a threat to the system.

That's why nobody smokes pot anymore—everybody's afraid of the freedom. They're afraid they're going to smoke some pot, get high, think a thought or two, realize what bullshit their life is . . . and freak out.

That's why I stopped making art, man. It's hopeless. What can you say about this situation?

You write a book, best book ever written, makes best-seller list, everybody reads it. Two months later it's forgotten, there's some other important book everybody's supposed to read. You write a song, beautiful song, makes Top 40. Next thing you know, it's a jingle in a beer commercial. You paint a painting, millionaire buys it, hangs it on the wall of his corporate headquarters.

In the old days, man, rich people used to get lions' heads and tigers' heads, hang 'em on the wall—made 'em feel powerful, made 'em feel safe.

The system collects artists' minds, man. It sleeps better at night knowing the best and the brightest are dead from the neck up.

That's why I don't give 'em the satisfaction. I keep my mind inside my head where they can't get at it. Everything becomes part of the system, man. The only way to escape the system is not to do anything.

That's what I do. I want to paint a painting, I want to write something, I do it in my head, where they can't see it.

If they ever knew what I was thinking, man . . . I'd be dead.

ORPHANS

I create more monologues than I can use in the process of building a show like *Sex, Drugs, Rock & Roll.*

I become very attached to some of them. What follow are my favorite "orphans."

BEAT POEM

*(A man wearing sunglasses speaks into a
microphone. His voice is resonant and hip.)*
    (Pause)

I open my eyes
to the ragged skies
of another hot city morning.
The sirens scream
the hookers dream
a beggar shouts a warning.
I know this place
I've been here before
it hasn't changed in a hundred years
of tears and beers and cheers and leers and
     fears
in the asphalt-covered, blood-encrusted,
     copper-jacketed,

broken-glass-ornamented highways and
    byways of a
never-never land called:
"take me out to the ball game, baby,"
honey-chile
suck my dick in the thick of the midnight
    fog
when the razors get sharpened
and the needles get filled
and the red flowers blossom
and the dragon's tail gets chased.
I know, I know
I know all about this place where the
    black leather buckles
and nooses go round and round and round
my arms and legs and necks and tongues
in the gray, gray cold dark beach sand
    morning
when the connection is closed and the
    night train's empty.
I know.
And I wake and I walk,
past hydrants gushing, cops reading,
    pigeons pecking,
bottle men digging,
past hustlers hustling and winos dying.
Past all that, past you, past me . . .

past the past and past the present.
I am the ancient insect trying to molt my
    skin and
find a new morning, but this morning . . .
"there's nothing happening, man!"
Like they say, like they say.
"To be or not to be—that *is* the
    question."
And then, and then . . .
A small piece of crumpled green paper on
    the ground.
Manna
Specie
Do-re-mi
A portrait of a President if you will.
Who knows who lost it?
Maybe some nine-to-five, square as a
    cornflakes box
capitalist slave to the oppressive red, white,
    and blue
Apache dance called America.
I don't know who lost the dough,
but I know who found it.
A member of the underclass
a member of the holy class
one of the knowing ones, one of the
    chosen ones

doomed to walk in the summer's heat
in search of powdered poppies.
Doomed to ride the white horse.
Sail the crystal ship.
Fly the magic carpet.
Me.
To be found, to be found, so that I am no
      longer lost!
And I find my man—
the heartless doctor who heals my soul,
      who gives me
my medicine.
And I take it and I
love it, cook it, smother it with my arms
      and
flesh and cells and blood.
Let it flow . . . let the tears of God flow
      into my arm.
Let the white mix with the red.
And then . . . and then . . .
This morning doesn't have to be broken
      glass and barnacles
sticking to the underside
of a long lost ghost ship of a life. . . .
But a morning like any other . . .
full of coffee and cigarettes
and newspapers

and corn
muffins. . . .
In the valley of the shadow of death . . .
my cup runneth over . . .
As the hydrants gush
as the sirens scream
as the hookers bop
as the junkie nods . . .
Forever
and forever
and forever. . . .
Amen.

FAIRY TALE

(A man speaks in a clean-cut-American accent.)

Used to be a time when this country was pretty great. A guy would get up in the morning, put on a nice pair of pressed pants and a starched white shirt, shave his face clean, comb his hair, eat a couple of fried eggs with bacon and toast, drink a cup of coffee, and go to work.

His wife would tend the children, who would be well behaved, and they'd all go to church together on Sundays.

A guy got a decent wage for an honest job; he owned his own home, washed the car on Saturdays, loved his wife, liked baseball, believed in the President, and prayed to God.

People valued simple things in their lives. They didn't want too much. They worked hard and stuck with their family and friends. They loved their children and they slept peacefully at night.

I feel like I'm telling you a fairy tale. But that's the way it used to be in America.

Of course, all of that was a long time ago. It was before television, and it was before rock and roll. It was before our defeat in Vietnam. It was before civil rights and before women's lib. Before gay liberation and before LSD. Before protest marches and before ecology.

Maybe next time, before we're so fast to change things, we should think about what we've got.

FOOD

(A man stands at a counter, making selections.)

Yes. . . . Tell me something—are the dried tomato raviolis made from dried tomatoes, or are they made with fresh tomatoes and then the ravioli is dried? . . . Do you know? . . . Could you ask someone? . . . Well, because I'm allergic to fresh tomatoes, but I can eat a dried tomato. Well, forget about that. The monkfish and arugula ravioli—tell me, what sort of fish is the monkfish? Is it an oily fish? . . . Well, like tuna or swordfish, as opposed to a whitefish like sole or scrod. I can't eat an oily fish. . . . You don't know that, either.

You don't know much, do you? Okay, well, just give me a dozen of the smoked mozzarella and Parma prosciutto ravioli, a dozen of the wild mushroom and Icelandic caviar and . . . um . . . the lobster and pesto ravioli—the lobster, is it Maine lobster or is it South

African lobster? . . . Maine lobster has the claws, South African lobster is just the tail. . . . I can't eat South African lobster, for obvious reasons. . . . The lobster . . . the lobster they make the ravioli out of . . . oh, never mind. Forget the lobster—just give me what I've ordered and . . . um . . . what's that? . . . Is it good? How much a pound? . . . Twenty-seven dollars a pound?! Give me three pounds. . . . And um . . . tell me, how are the kalamata olives today? . . . Well, are they too salty? Sometimes they're too salty. . . . Just give me a pound. And do you know if you carry those little goat cheese and Spanish avocado pies? . . . Well, no, they're not a quiche—they're more like a tart . . . um, they used to have them at Montrachet, and then the chef left and— . . . Um . . . no, they're not key lime pie. . . . No, not chocolate—did I say chocolate? I said goat cheese! . . . I don't know! If I knew how to make them, I would make them myself, wouldn't I? Listen, all right, forget about the pies, it's okay, it's okay. Just, uh, give me the ravioli, the olives, the pâté, and, um . . . five pounds of the Royal Blue Jamaican coffee beans—don't grind them, please . . . *No, don't grind them!* Do you have trouble with your hearing? You should get it checked. Let me see. . . . What else? What else do I need? That's it—just give me two heads of radicchio lettuce and a Dutch yellow pepper. . . . What? I have to go over *there* to get the vegetables?

But I'm here—there's a long line over there. Can't you get it for me? . . . I can see you're busy—you're busy waiting on *me!* And I really don't want to go stand in line over there—please go over and get my vegetables.

No, I don't want to speak to the manager, I will go over myself, but I want you to know that I purchase at least a hundred dollars' worth of groceries here every three or four days, and I should think that you would make some effort to assist a regular customer. But I guess that's asking too much, isn't it? You have more important things to do.

I'm not angry—there's nothing I'm saying that should make you think I'm angry. I'm simply pointing out that you should make more of an effort. . . . I DON'T WANT TO GO OVER THERE! I DON'T HAVE THE TIME. I'M TOO BUSY—CAN'T YOU SEE THAT, YOU IDIOT! SOME OF US HAVE MORE IMPORTANT THINGS TO DO THAN HANG AROUND ALL DAY, BUT I GUESS YOU WOULDN'T KNOW WHAT I'M TALKING ABOUT, WOULD YOU? NO. . . . I'm fine, it's fine—just give me the bag, and thank you . . . thank you for your help. Thank you very much. Thank you very much, you've been most helpful . . . I can't tell you what a great help you've been. . . . Thank you. You too. Merry Christmas to you too. . . .

RASH FINAL

(A man, seated, is talking animatedly.)

But George, that's the whole point! It's making me a nervous wreck! I saw a guy come up to another guy on the street yesterday and start pushing him. . . . No, he wasn't Black, but he was big. . . . So he starts pushing him, and the next thing I know the guy who's getting pushed starts karate-chopping the big guy! Just keeps hitting him!

(Looking up)

Oh, yes . . . *(Picks up menu)* Ummm . . . What was the special fish of the day? . . . Monkfish? What's that? Is that an oily fish? I can't eat an oily fish. . . . It comes with capers? I hate capers. . . . What's this? The avocado and wild raspberry ravioli? Is it any good?

. . . You don't know? The dried tomato ravioli—is that
made from dried tomatoes or is the ravioli dried?
. . . No . . . no . . . don't check, it's okay. . . . George,
what are you having? . . . The monkfish? There's nothing to eat here. . . . All right . . . well, give me the
lobster. . . . Yes . . . now, wait—is that a Maine lobster
or a South African lobster? I can't eat South African
lobster. . . . Maine lobster comes with the claws.
. . . Claws *(Indicates)* . . . Look, forget it, just give me
the monkfish—but can you make it without capers and
grilled, no butter. *Comprende? Con* butter? . . . Fine,
and yes, we'll both have the arugula salad, but could
you leave the radicchio out of mine? Thanks. . . . No,
no wine, we don't drink, just, uh . . . a bottle of San
Pellegrino—and George, you want another Diet Coke?
Two more Diet Cokes. . . .

It's crazy. . . . Listen to this. Every day when I go
out for lunch I walk by this beggar on Lexington Avenue, right? Same guy, he's there every day, so every day
I give him a quarter, just doing my thing, right? So
about a month ago, I'm out to get my lunch, and I see
the guy, crouched down next to this building. So I
reach into my pocket to get out a quarter and I don't
have any change! All I have is a dollar bill, so I'm
thinking, "I can't give this guy a buck, he'll be follow-
ing me for the rest of my life." But then I see that he
sees me and he's watching me, so I figure, "All right,

give him the buck, and walk on the other side of the street for a month or so until he forgets you."

So I hand him the buck, and the next thing I know he's reaching up for my hand, shaking my hand, thanking me, right? And for the first time I get a good look at the guy, and I mean, George, he's really awful. I mean, he's got no teeth, he's got bloody sores all over his face, horrible. And he's blessing me and thanking me and he won't let go of my hand. I'm thinking, "I hope no one from the office comes by—they'll see me with this guy and think I'm buying drugs or something," right? So I pull my hand away and I go and pick up a sandwich at the deli. . . .

Fine . . . I—oh, waiter! Could you bring us some more bread, please? . . . The sourdough, yes, that's fine. . . . So I get back to my office, and normally whenever I walk into the office I go right into the john and wash my hands—you know, if I've been on the subway or something, you never know what you might pick up. Well, I walk in the door and Sandy's freaking out because the fax machine is smoking and we have this big job to get out and no one can figure out what to do but me. So we run the job next door, and I forget to wash my hands!

Three days later I start to get this rash between my fingers. Little red pimples . . . and it's spreading up my hand! I'm thinking it's poison ivy I picked up at the country house, but then I figure it out . . . it's the guy! The bum, the beggar! He touched me! I got some kind of bum disease!

So I have to go to the doctor, I'm there all day, lose a day's work, a hundred and twenty bucks for cortisone shots and cortisone cream, and, George, I'm telling you, what's the point? You see what I'm saying? You try to help somebody out and look what happens? I mean, I was going to volunteer for one of those . . . those volunteer things, but now I realize, what's the use? It's like carrying coals to Newcastle.

I don't even want to be in the city anymore. It's too depressing. I'm just going to move my whole operation up to the country house . . . I just feel so much better up there! I mean, all I need is the phone and the fax machine—let Sandy commute up to me. . . . Oh, yeah, the town doesn't mind my doing business there, as long as you don't build on less than five acres. . . .

Thank you . . . that looks very nice. . . . No, no ground pepper for me—but could you get me some margarine, when you get a chance?

The next town over from ours lets you build on anything, even a quarter of an acre. It's horrible over there: rusty cars sitting in the front lawn, children running around with dogs. But I guess those people have to live somewhere. . . . And my town is so nice, the people are so nice. We've even got together and bought some vacant land in the center of town and we're going to build a recycling center and start an organic garden. We'll probably end up donating the food to the next town. . . .

But enough depressing talk—let's eat. . . .

What? Oh, the rash? Went away in three days. But you wanna hear the weird thing? That guy I gave the dollar to? He disappeared as well—somebody in the office said they heard he died. . . .

Could you pass the San Pellegrino? Thanks.

MEDICINE

(A man walks out from behind a desk, very relaxed, congenial, slightly patronizing.)

David, come in, sit down. Sit down. You look good. How are you feeling? . . . Good. Have a seat.

Well, we've gotten the results back from the lab and they're good, they're good, lots of positive indicators. I'll give you a copy of the report to take home.

Now I think to be on the safe side, we should start to get into a little treatment . . . okay?

Basically, what I'm gonna do is, David, is I'm gonna put you on a little medication here.

I'm going to write you a couple of prescriptions. And we'll just, uh, see how it goes. I can't say it's gonna do anything, but it won't hurt, either.

Now this stuff is strong. It does have a few side effects. I just want you to know what they are, so if anything does come up that you don't get overly concerned.

(Writes on a prescription pad)

Now, first of all, let me ask you this, David—do you drink milk? . . . Well, like in your cereal or in your morning coffee . . . any baked products with milk in them. . . . Stay away from milk, that's the first thing you'll want to do. Milk and eggs. Don't eat any eggs, either. . . .

Well, because . . . the amino acids present in milk and eggs can react with the medication and in some cases can . . . well, they can cause seizures. And we don't want that, do we? We want you getting better, not worse. So, no milk or eggs.

(Writes some more)

Now after about a week on the medication you may notice some blurring of vision. That will clear up in a few days. Don't worry about it—just means the medicine is working. Another thing that we've noticed is that your sex drive will be diminished, you won't have a . . . uh . . . normal sex drive. . . . Well, uh, to a great degree. . . . I'd be surprised if you have any sex drive at all. . . .

Ummm . . . you might also get a little dizzy when you stand up, but don't worry about that. What you will find worrisome is when you're showering, uh, sometimes you'll be losing some hair. Clumps of air. Again, this is perfectly normal, if a bit unsightly. If you're having a problem with this, I would prescribe—well, I would prescribe a hat. Something like that can clear that right up.

Also, it's very common after a couple of weeks to start getting some itching. You might even get what we call an epidermal sebaceous trauma, just a fancy term for a large scab. That's all. Just a large bleeding scab. You'll get them on your arms and on your legs. That's what this second prescription is for, it's just some cortisone cream to reduce the swelling and itching.

You will also notice some numbness in your fingers and your toes, your nose, your ears, all your extremities.

And after a month, how shall I say this, you will experience some temporary blindness. It's only temporary. Usually when you get up in the morning you just can't see for a few minutes. It really has no clinical significance.

And we find in nine out of ten cases, patients are aware of frequent nausea. Also when you're getting up in the morning: nausea, vomiting, incontinence. . . . If you find you're having a problem holding your bowels, I can give you a prescription for that too, clear it right up.

And I tell all my patients using this medication to try and keep your meals small so that you don't interfere with your nutrition when you vomit. . . .

Bleeding . . . your nose will bleed from time to time. The first time it happens, it can be kind of funny, because you don't expect it. You'll be having a meal with friends and suddenly you'll see drops of blood on your plate. It can be embarrassing. Just make sure you keep a handkerchief handy. And should you get a nosebleed, just hold your head back and dab. Gently. But don't blow. That's the worst thing. Just dab. It'll clear up in around five or ten minutes.

And . . . um . . . that's it. . . . And after a couple of months we'll run some more tests, see how the medication is doing. If we don't get the results we want, we'll try something stronger. Okay?

David, it was nice seeing you. . . .

(He stands, puts out his hand.)

Oh, don't thank me, it's just the miracle of modern medicine! *(Laughs at his own joke)*

And David—that insurance claim did come back, so could you drop a check by the front desk on your way out? Thanks. Take care now. . . .

ABOUT THE AUTHOR

Eric Bogosian is the author of *Drinking in America*, the book and play, and *Talk Radio*, which was a book, a play, and an Oliver Stone film. He has won two Obie Awards, a Silver Bear Award from the Berlin Film Festival, and a Drama Desk Award. *Sex, Drugs, Rock & Roll*, based on his play (and including new material), is his third book and is being released by Avenue Pictures as a motion picture. Born in Boston, Bogosian lives in New York City.